101 American Customs

101 American Customs

Harry Collis
Illustrated by Joe Kohl

PASSPORT BOOKS

NTC/Contemporary Publishing Group

Library of Congress Cataloging-in-Publication Data

Collis, Harry.
  101 English customs : understanding language and culture through
common practices / Harry Collis ; illustrated by Joe Kohl.
     p.   cm.
  ISBN 0-8442-2407-3
     1. United States—Social life and customs—1971–   2. Language and
culture—United States.   3. English language—Study and teaching—Foreign
speakers.   I. Title.   II. Title: One hundred and one American English
customs.   III. Title: One hundred one American English customs.
E169.04.C647   1999
306.44′0973—dc21   99-29186
                                                                         CIP

Other titles in this series:

101 American English Idioms
101 American English Proverbs
101 American English Riddles
101 American Superstitions

Published by Passport Books,
a division of NTC/Contemporary Publishing Group, Inc.,
4255 West Touhy Avenue,
Lincolnwood (Chicago), Illinois 60712-1975 U.S.A.
© 2000 by NTC/Contemporary Publishing Group, Inc.
Manufactured in the United States of America.
International Standard Book Number: 0-8442-2407-3

1 2 3 4 5 6 7 8 9 RRC 9 8 7 6 5 4 3

Contents

Foreword   vii

Acknowledgments   ix

Part 1:
Those Special Occasions   1
A Visit from the Stork • Blue Is for Boys—Pink Is for Girls • Passing
Out Cigars • Baptism • Singing Happy Birthday • Birthday
Spankings • The Birthday Cake and Candles • First Communion •
Bar Mitzvah • The Sweet Sixteen Party • Hazing • Caps and Gowns
at Graduation • The Homecoming Parade • Going with a Date to the
Prom • The Retirement Watch • Sending Greeting Cards

Part 2:
Courtship and Marriage   19
Marking X for Kisses • Spin the Bottle • Parking with a Date • Going
Dutch • The Sadie Hawkins Dance • Asking for a Woman's Hand •
Bridal Showers • Bachelor Parties • The Bride's Family Paying for
the Wedding • "You May Kiss The Bride" • Throwing Rice at
Newlyweds • Cutting the Wedding Cake • Anniversary Gifts

Part 3:
Body Language   35
Shaking Hands • The "OK" Sign • Thumbs Up—Thumbs Down • The
High Five • Crossing Your Fingers • Crossing Your Heart •
Shrugging Your Shoulders • Winking • Sticking Out Your Tongue •
A Hand over the Mouth When Yawning • Saying "Bless You" When
Sneezing • The Man Walks on the Outside

Part 4:
Enjoy!   49
Giving Thanks Before a Meal • Keeping Elbows off the Table •
Cornflakes for Breakfast • Bacon and Eggs • Having Salad Before the
Entrée • TV Dinners • Ketchup, the American Flavor Marker • The
Backyard Barbecue • Potluck Dinners • Eating Fish on Friday •
Drive-Thru Fast Food • Hot Dogs at a Baseball Game

Part 5:

All in the Family 63

Fall Shopping Sprees • Kiss It and Make It Better • Regular
Toothbrushing • The Tooth Fairy • Sibling Rivalry • The Weekly
Allowance • Bedtime Stories • An Apple for the Teacher • Separate
Phone Lines for Teens • Coupon Clipping • Garage Sales •
Tupperware Parties • Spring Cleaning • Church Collections

Part 6:

Let's Have Fun! 79

A Game of Bingo • Square Dancing • Going to a Rodeo • Demolition
Derbies • A Visit to the Amusement Park or Theme Park • Eating
Contests • TGIF (Thank Goodness It's Friday) • Tailgate Parties •
Baseball—America's Game • Playing on Little League Teams •
Listening to One's Favorite Music • Lighting Matches at a Rock
Concert

Part 7:

Red Letter Days 93

Honoring Martin Luther King's Birthday • Celebrating Mardi Gras •
Presidents' Day Sales • Wearing Green on Saint Patrick's Day •
Sending Flowers on Mother's Day • Wearing a Poppy for Memorial
Day • Independence Day Parade • "Trick or Treat" on Halloween •
Voting on Election Day • Gathering for Thanksgiving Dinner •
Celebrating Kwanza

Part 8:

The Icons of America 107

Visiting the Statue of Liberty • Taking in a Broadway Show •
Stargazing in Hollywood • Enjoying Popcorn at the Movies •
Ordering an Ice-Cream Cone • Chewing Gum • Having a Coke • The
Morning Cup of Coffee • As American as Apple Pie • Wearing Blue
Jeans • Reading Personal Advice Columns

Index 121

Foreword

Have you ever wondered why Americans say "cross my heart and hope to die," why they shake hands, why Catholics eat fish on Friday, why Americans throw rice at weddings, or why they dress boys in blue and girls in pink? *101 American Customs* seeks out the answers to these questions by exploring the backgrounds of the customs that are sanctioned rituals of contemporary American society.

Arriving at someone else's doorstep with little or no knowledge of its government, religion, history, or national character is no way for the newcomer to America to hit a "home run" with his or her American hosts. An accepted gesture, a greeting, or an act of generosity in one culture might well be considered gauche or even rude in another. Do not expect to shake hands with a woman accompanying a Saudi, or even to be introduced to her. The widely accepted American "OK" sign is considered vulgar or obscene in Brazil, and is considered impolite in Greece and in the former Soviet Union. Although Japanese coming to the West make the concession of shaking hands, they feel more at home with the traditional bow, which many Americans regard as out-and-out kowtowing. Waving in Greece is a serious insult. A culinary delight in one culture (sheep's eyes, bear's paw soup, or a roast gorilla hand) might be completely rejected in another. What would an American think of a newcomer who refused a piece of homemade apple pie or a sizzling sirloin? Thus, a knowledge of the habits and mores of one culture is the key that opens the door to the understanding and appreciation of another.

101 American Customs is designed to provide the newcomer with insights into what Americans say and do while at work, at worship, and at play. The book is divided into eight thematic sections in order to help the reader understand the focus of the particular customs. It is hoped that the backgrounds and dialogues of the entries will provide the reader with the necessary tools to hit a "home run" with his or her American hosts.

Acknowledgments

I should like to express my profound appreciation to my wife, Katherine, for her patience and understanding in the realization of this project.

I am particularly grateful to my grandson, Adam Jennison, and to my daughter, Denise Jennison, for their inspired input to the narratives and dialogues of the manuscript.

My appreciation also goes to my colleague, Dr. Susan Larkin, for her valuable contributions in the writing of several of the scenarios.

My deep thanks also go to the director of my English Institute, Susan Pendo, and to my co-workers, Diane Gonzales and Lisa Bell, for their constant support and incisive suggestions.

101 American Customs

Part 1
Those Special Occasions

1 A Visit from the Stork

Several factors contributed to the belief in the stork as the bringer of babies. People watched the stork take care in making its home, and they noted how out of devotion it returned to the same spot each year. Also, the storks love water, and tradition held that it was in watery places that the souls of the unborn children dwelt.

A: Hi, Al. Heard you had a visit from the stork the other day.
B: Sure did! A bouncing baby boy! I've got to admit—the doctor deserves some of the credit, too.

2 Blue Is for Boys— Pink Is for Girls

Since all babies look alike, boys are usually dressed in blue and girls in pink simply to identify the sex. In ancient times, girl babies were regarded as inferior to boy babies, so the color blue, which was believed to have the power to ward off evil spirits, was reserved exclusively for the boys. The color pink was introduced for baby girls in accordance with a legendary European tradition that suggested girls were born inside a pink rose.

A: What color are you going to paint the baby's room?

B: I'm not too sure. It all depends if we're having a boy or girl.

A: How about yellow? It's sunny and bright, and it'll fit a baby of either sex.

B: Good idea! And I won't have to repaint if we have twins—a girl for you and a boy for me.

3 Passing Out Cigars

In primitive ceremonies an individual blessed with the arrival of a baby shared his fortune with the community, to avoid the envy of both his fellows and the gods. The smoke of a proud papa's pipe drifting toward the heavens was a sort of appeasement to the heavenly powers. Today's father's distribution of cigars to celebrate the arrival of a baby may be regarded as a modern variant of this ritual.

A: Wow! Those are prime cigars! Where did you get them?

B: Actually, I got them from a friend. He's been passing them out right and left. His wife just gave birth.

A: Oh, what did she have—a boy or a girl?

B: She had triplets! Why do you think I have so many cigars?

4 Baptism

From ancient times water served the dual purpose of purifying and protecting both mother and child from evil spirits. The Christian notion is that the water washes away original sin. Thus, in the Christian baptismal ceremony the child is either immersed in the baptismal basin (as in the Greek Orthodox ceremony) or sprinkled with holy water (as in the Catholic ceremony). The Christian baptism also includes the naming of the child, since during the baptismal rite the child is reborn into Christ.

A: Did you receive an invitation to the baptism of Todd's daughter?

B: Yup. It's this Sunday, right?

A: Right. And he's having a party afterward. Will you be coming?

B: Sure will. How could I ever pass up those delicacies that his wife always prepares on occasions like this?

5 Singing Happy Birthday

The original title of the song was "Good Morning to You," and it was written in the late nineteenth century by two sisters involved in elementary education. They composed a song with a simple melody and lyrics that even a child of three could sing without hesitation.

A: (Invited guests singing) . . . Happy birthday, dear Carol. Happy birthday to you!

B: Mom, I'd sure like to see what's in that big box before we have our cake and ice cream.

C: You'll have to be patient just a little while longer so we can open all the presents at the same time. You know, good things come in small packages, too.

6 Birthday Spankings

The mock spanking administered to a birthday boy or girl recalls a rite that has long been an integral feature of many initiation ceremonies. The "public" spanking highlights the specialness of the child and invites the child back into the fold by offering him or her luck (one to grow on) and congratulations.

A: I can hardly wait. My birthday is coming up in two more days.
B: (Jokingly) Will you still be getting your little birthday spanking to wish you luck and an extra one to grow on?
A: Get serious! Sure, Mom and Dad always pretended to "pat" my behind and tell me that I needed an extra one to grow on when I was growing up. But I'm already six feet, two inches tall. Does it look like I need to grow any more?

7 The Birthday Cake and Candles

With each birthday, Americans not only celebrate growth but also the passing of another year. Thus, candles are symbols of both life and death, as well as both hope and fear. When a person makes a wish over these symbols, he or she invokes powers for good fortune. And when that person snuffs out these symbols, he or she expresses the hope to have a degree of control over whatever lies in store for him or her.

A: Happy birthday! Now close your eyes, make a wish, and blow out the candles.

B: (The birthday girl blows out all of the candles at once.)

A: Hooray for you! You blew them all out in one breath. That means you'll get your wish for sure.

B: But, Dad. You said that you wouldn't allow me to have a chimpanzee as a pet around the house.

A: Oops!

8 First Communion

The First Holy Communion, a Roman Catholic religious
ceremony, has its origins in the Middle Ages, when
children had to understand the distinction between plain
bread and the bread of life (the body of Christ) before
they were given Communion. Now church leaders accept
seven or eight years old as an age of reason when the
children (often dressed in white) receive their First Holy
Communion, without requiring the children to explain
the distinction between the two breads.

A: Where are you off to, Sally?
B: I'm going to my confirmation class tonight. I have my First
Communion next Sunday. My parents are having a get-together for
family and friends after the ceremony. Why don't you drop by?
A: Don't mind if I do. And I'll bring a little something for you to make
your day even more rewarding.
B: Only if you insist.

9 Bar Mitzvah

The bar mitzvah (a Hebrew term referring to the ceremony of marking one as a son of the commandment) occurs on the day after a Jewish boy's thirteenth birthday. According to Jewish law, thirteen is considered the age of responsibility for boys. At the bar mitzvah the boy is required to give the congregation a public address to emphasize his coming of age. The opening line for such a speech is: "Today I am a man." A similar ceremony, the bat mitzvah, marks the passage of a girl to womanhood.

The day of Josh's bar mitzvah was indeed a joyous occasion. After having spent many hours studying the Torah and preparing his public address for the congregation, Josh felt that he was indeed ready to declare that he was a man. Now, as a young man ready to assume responsibilities, he was assigned the task of warmly greeting the guests, who had been invited to the reception that his parents had planned for this special day.

10 The Sweet Sixteen Party

Since the number sixteen is said to represent the midpoint of the teen years, a "sweet sixteen" party has served as a kind of puberty initiation rite, particularly for girls. The expression "sweet sixteen and never been kissed," although perhaps not as true today as in earlier times, is still alive and serves as a theme for many parties celebrating the teen years.

A: Did you have a good birthday, Nancy?

B: Boy, was I ever embarrassed! We went out to dinner, and when my dad told the waiters it was my sixteenth birthday, they all sang "Happy Birthday" to me, and then one by one, they gave me a little kiss on the cheek.

A: Well, you know the old saying, "sweet sixteen and never been kissed." I guess they didn't want to see you miss out.

B: But I'm fine. I already have a boyfriend.

11 Hazing

Hazing, the submitting of initiates to indignities at the
hands of upperclassmen, is a part of a tradition of rites of
passage. As a pledging rite, the freshmen, or fraternity
pledges, prove their worthiness to be members of that
particular body, by partaking in and going along with
ridiculous, self-debasing acts. By doing so they show that
they can and will confirm to the authority that governs
that body.

A: What's Hal doing in a bunny suit?
B: Don't you know? He is a pledge to join a fraternity, and he's going
   through hazing.
A: Man, I guess I'll never join a frat. I'm not ever going to let
   somebody make such a fool out of me.
B: Perish the thought. You're doing fine all by yourself!

12 Caps and Gowns at Graduation

In medieval Europe the caps and gowns worn by the academic community were in black. The color black, the preference of ecclesiastical leaders, was a symbol of authority. This austerity has been retained by modern high schools and universities in the caps and gowns worn at graduation ceremonies. The tassel that graduates transfer from one side of the cap to the other as a sign of their elevation is an outgrowth of the medieval biretta, a tufted square cap appropriated by undergraduates and schoolboys.

A: Hi, Jane. Graduation is next week. Have you rented your cap and gown yet?

B: You bet! My mom and dad have been taking pictures of me wearing them all week.

A: What do you do to keep your cap on? Mine falls off every time I look up.

B: No problem. Use bobby pins and always look down. You never know what you'll find.

A: Come on, be serious!

13 The Homecoming Parade

Homecoming is an event held every fall by many high schools and colleges, especially in small towns. It is a weeklong celebration with parties, dances, and dinners for the old graduates (alumni), as well as for the new students and their friends and parents. One of the outstanding events is the crowning of the homecoming queen, who is chosen by the students of the school. The queen rides in parades and opens the sports event—usually a homecoming football game.

A: Who are you voting for to be homecoming queen and king?
B: Well, I'll probably vote for the football captain for king, but I don't know who should be queen.
A: Why not vote for his girlfriend Mary? Then they can be in the homecoming parade and go to the homecoming dance together.
B: Good idea. They make a great couple!

14 Going with a Date to the Prom

The prom is a very special high school dance that is held in the spring. This formal occasion is usually for the third- and fourth-year students. The boys and girls go to the dance in elegant attire, and dance away the evening to the music of a live band.

A: How was your prom?

B: I had a great time! I wore a pink evening gown and Sam brought me an orchid corsage. We had dinner at a fancy French restaurant, and then off we went to the prom and danced until two in the morning.

A: Sounds fantastic! I sure hope that I have as good a time at my prom. The only problem in my case is that my parents really get upset when I stay out too late.

B: There should be no reason to worry—as long as you're with a guy they trust.

15 The Retirement Watch

The retirement watch, an engraved timepiece, is often given to a retiree as a reward for years of service to a firm. In the nineteenth century the common laborer, not being able to afford the jeweled timepiece of the upper class, nevertheless satisfied his desire for status by acquiring a pocket watch with an engraved lid and dangling chain. It could function as a testimonial to both the owner's ability to tell time and the fact that he was on his way up the social ladder.

A: Why does Dad look so depressed?

B: Well, you know, he retired last week. Last night his company threw a retirement party for him and gave him an engraved watch. Now all he can say is that he has no reason to wear the watch, because he doesn't have anyplace to go anymore.

16 Sending Greeting Cards

The custom of sending greeting cards to friends and relatives for special occasions originated in England, where the practice was limited to people who could afford to pay private messengers to carry their greetings across great distances. With the advent of a British law that established inexpensive mail delivery, a market for sending greeting cards for birthdays, anniversaries—almost any occasion imaginable—opened up overnight. In America the card market was expanded by the founder of Hallmark Cards, whose company led the way in other products of social expression such as gift wrap, stationery, and calendars.

A: We have to get Susan a card.

B: What's the occasion?

A: She had her baby last night—a little girl.

B: Super! Let's get her a baby stroller, and we can all sign the card.

A: Okay. Let's send her some flowers with a nice card for now, and we can surprise her with the stroller when she gets home. She's going to need all the rest she can get.

Part 2
Courtship and Marriage

17 Marking X for Kisses

The use of an *X* at the end of a letter to signify a kiss goes back to the Middle Ages, when an illiterate person signed his or her name to marked documents and contracts with an *X* (which in church lore stands for Christ) and kissed the mark in the presence of witnesses to affirm his or her sincerity. The kiss and the cross became synonymous, and this early link has now become a universal shorthand of love and affection.

A: Boy, am I ever excited!

B: How come?

A: Well, I just got a letter from Sally.

B: So?

A: So? She signed off with a bunch of *X*'s, and here I thought it was all over with us.

18 Spin the Bottle

Spin the bottle is a kissing game that has been popular in American culture. In this game a participant must spin an empty bottle and kiss the person the spun bottle points to. This game is popular especially among teenagers, because it allows contact with the opposite sex without having to get really personal.

A: What a ball we had playing spin the bottle at Steve's party!
B: Was Liz there?
A: Yup. But don't sweat it. I know you two are going steady. You'll be relieved to know that she didn't play along.
B: That's comforting, but I'd still like to know what she was doing there.

19 Parking with a Date

Parking, or "roadside kissing," was practiced in the horse-and-buggy days and was further abetted by the advent of the automobile. Parking, leading to erotic interactions between the partners, provided sexually awakening adolescents with an outlet for physical desires. Although quite widespread in the 1950s, parking is still popular with the young people of today.

A: I hear you were out with Louise the other night. How did it go?

B: Well, I was all set to park up at Twin Peaks, but things didn't turn out the way I hoped they would.

A: What happened? Didn't she want to go and admire the starry sky?

B: Don't be funny! It was past her curfew, and she asked me to drop her off at her house instead.

A: What a bummer!

20 Going Dutch

The linking of the word *Dutch* with such expressions as "Dutch bargain" (an uneven, one-sided deal), "Dutch reckoning" (an unitemized account), "Dutch courage" (bravery induced by drink), and "double Dutch" (unintelligible gibberish) stems from the time when the Dutch and the English were mercantile and military rivals, and when the English characterized all things Dutch as nothing but shams. Thus, "going Dutch" or "Dutch treat" (splitting expenses with a date) was to mimic the behavior of those "strange" people across the Channel.

It's easy to understand why William has so much trouble holding on to any of his girlfriends. After all, when he asks a girl out on a date and then insists that they go Dutch to dinner and to the movies, it's no wonder that girls think twice before going out with him again.

21 The Sadie Hawkins Dance

The Sadie Hawkins or Turnabout Dance is a high school dance where the girl gets to invite the boy. This custom stems from a fictional cartoon celebration known as Sadie Hawkins Day. On this day the unmarried women (Sadie Hawkins, the unattractive daughter of the mayor, being one of them) were allowed to run after a man of their choice. Each man caught by a woman would return to town for a shotgun wedding. A similar time when women can initiate aggressive action is during the leap year, when February has twenty-nine days. According to this custom, on leap day, February 29, a woman can propose marriage to a man.

The Sadie Hawkins dance at Fairmont High School was quite successful. With the girls inviting the boys, it turned out that each young lady would have a dancing partner for the entire evening so there would be no young ladies waiting anxiously to be invited to dance. After the dance, however, the boys ended up paying for the hamburgers and french fries.

22 Asking for a Woman's Hand

The tradition of a man asking for a woman's hand dates back to a Roman marriage custom in which the father "let go" of his daughter and transferred her to the hand of her husband. An equivalent of the "letting go" custom can be seen in the modern marriage ceremony, where the father gives the bride away.

You could have knocked Fernando over with a feather when Mariana's dad not only gave the future bride and groom his blessing, but offered to foot the bill for the wedding reception as well.

23 Bridal Showers

Bridal showers are given by close friends of the bride-to-be as a sort of dowry to start the bride off on her forthcoming role as a wife. The shower gifts are usually of the domestic variety, such as linens and kitchen utensils. These gifts are a "prelude" to the more expensive gifts that will be given at the wedding.

A: Diane, I can't thank you enough for the bridal shower you had for me!

B: My pleasure! You really got some lovely gifts. Those kitchen utensils will sure come in handy.

A: Well, I guess I'll now have to learn how to cook.

24 Bachelor Parties

Bachelor parties (also referred to as stag parties) are prewedding bachelor dinners that originated in Sparta, where the dinner was called a "men's mess." This party is an integral part of the prewedding ceremony when the young single man wishes to bid farewell to his buddies. In America the party tends to become very noisy with an emphasis on getting the groom drunk and entertaining him with off-color humor.

A: Hey, Newton! How did it go at Fred's bachelor party?
B: We had a great time! Let me just say, it's a good thing none of us was married.

25 The Bride's Family Paying for the Wedding

The cost of the wedding can be viewed as an outgrowth of the dowry custom. In societies where the groom had to pay for his bride, the dowry served as a "return gift." Although the compensating value of the dowry no longer exists in modern America, the father of the bride mirrors the ancient system of marital payback by paying for the wedding.

A: I heard that Dorothy's folks paid a bundle for the wedding.
B: Yeah! Her dad is really loaded. You should have seen all the guests!
A: Mostly from the bride's side, I bet.

26 "You May Kiss the Bride"

Kissing as means of expressing affection appears to have developed more extensively in Western cultures than in Eastern ones. The kiss at the end of the wedding ceremony is believed to be an expression of bride and groom's true selves and an affirmation of their devotion for each other.

Jack and Jill were truly made for each other. Who could have thought anything else after having witnessed that long kiss at the end of their wedding ceremony? Here it is twenty years later and they're still acting like newlyweds!

27 Throwing Rice at Newlyweds

The custom of throwing rice at newlyweds derives from a pagan rite of showering the happy couple with grain. A Roman wife was married with wheat sheaves and, with her husband, ate a postceremonial cake made of wheat. The wheat sheaf and cake were meant to impel bliss and to ensure fertility, since it was believed that the fertility of the seeds would be transferred to the pair on whom they fell.

A: I must say that I admire Sarah's fortitude. With four kids and another on the way, I don't know how she does it.

B: I know what you mean. Do you suppose that shower of rice at the wedding might have helped things along?

A: Who knows? There might be something to that old belief that the fertility of the rice is transferred to the wedded couple.

B: It appears that Sarah is living proof that it's true.

28 Cutting the Wedding Cake

The cutting of the wedding cake represents a ritual that was seen as a dramatization of the male's dominance. At first, the groom directs the bride's hand to cut the first piece as proof of her submissiveness. The bride then offers the groom the first bite, symbolizing the partaking of her body. Then, as an act of revolt, she pushes the cake into her husband's face; however, he endures all without losing face. Finally, showing that she is obedient to her husband's wiser judgment, the bride wipes the icing from his face. Nowadays, most couples do not go through this ritual, and consider the cutting of the cake more as good luck for the marriage.

A: Here, Ralph, this first piece of the cake is for you. Take a bite and let me know what you think.

B: I will, but be careful not to get any of that frosting on me.

A: Don't worry. I don't want people to think we've had our first disagreement!

B: Cool!

29 Anniversary Gifts

The reason behind assigning traditional gift listings to anniversaries was that happiness deserved a reward. The greater the stability of the marriage, the greater the reward. Thus, the first year of marriage is celebrated with paper, while the fiftieth and sixtieth are celebrated with gold and a diamond respectively.

A: So, did you do anything exciting on your sixtieth anniversary?
B: We had a marvelous evening! Bob took me out to dinner and surprised me with a beautiful diamond ring. And how did yours go?
A: Oh, it slipped Greg's mind—again!

Part 3
Body Language

30 Shaking Hands

Shaking hands is a polite gesture indicating friendship and acceptance. At one time, however, meeting with a stranger aroused suspicion and fear. To prevent each other from suddenly attacking, strangers joined right hands as a pledge of nonaggression, thus demonstrating that neither party was about to use a weapon. Handshaking is now an activity practiced by both men and women not only to greet one another, but to seal a contract as well.

A: We've finally agreed on the price of the car. Right?
B: Absolutely!
A: Okay. Let's shake on that to seal the bargain.
B: Fine, no problem. All you have to do is sign the final papers and you can drive off and be on your way.

31 The "OK" Sign

The American "OK" sign, the joining of the thumb and forefinger in a circle, indicates that all is well or perfect. The OK sign acquired its modern connotation from the ancient world, wherein the circle itself was one of the oldest and most common symbols for perfection. The verbal expression "OK" is native to the United States and was formed in support of the letter *O* indicating that something was as perfect as a circle.

A: Look. I'll help you with your English paper if you help me with my math. This problem really has me stumped.

B: (Signaling consent with the "OK" sign) Great! First, check out my paper for grammar and spelling. The math problem should be a breeze!

A: Oh yeah? It might be a breeze for you, but it's more like a hurricane to me.

32 Thumbs Up— Thumbs Down

When not used in hitchhiking, the thumbs-up gesture in American culture typically indicates approval, while the thumbs-down gesture indicates disapproval. The gesture has been linked to the time of the Roman arena, where the emperor or mob supposedly ordered life or death for a gladiator by turning thumbs up or thumbs down.

After months of negotiating the terms of the contract for the construction of the new corporate headquarters, the president of the board finally gave the thumbs-up sign for the construction to begin. The company's acceptance of the contract would mean a plethora of jobs for contractors and workers alike.

33 The High Five

The slapping of the raised right hand with the open palm of another person's right hand is a pervasive gesture in American culture that indicates enthusiastic approval and acceptance of a deed or incident. This gesture may have sprung from the old Roman gesture of raising the right arm in praise or tribute to the emperor.

When the school team won the city championship in basketball, the students and teachers alike showed their elation by giving high fives to anyone they happened to encounter.

34 Crossing Your Fingers

Crossing one's fingers serves as protection from bad luck or from the penalties associated with lying. Thus, when people wish for good luck, they cross their fingers, and when they wish not to be held accountable for a lie, they cross their fingers and hide their arms behind their backs to not let on that they are lying.

A: My goodness, Ellen. I must say you look very nice today. What's the occasion?

B: I'm on my way to an interview for that management job. Keep your fingers crossed! I'll need all the luck I can get.

A: You got it! Let me know how things turn out.

35 Crossing Your Heart

Americans cross their hearts to seal promises or pledges.
Crossing the heart goes back to the religious tradition of
crossing oneself, which still exists in the Roman Catholic
and Orthodox churches. It is believed that the gesture
provides protection against bad luck by invoking the
power of this religious tradition, and thus attests that
the speaker's pledge is in earnest. Hence, the solemn
caution: "Cross my heart and hope to die," that is, if the
pledge proves to be false.

A: Are you sure you're going to make it to my party next weekend?
B: Cross my heart. I wouldn't miss it for anything in the world.
A: You'd better not! Jenny said she'd be there, too.
B: Well, that cinches it!

36 Shrugging Your Shoulders

In American culture shrugging the shoulders can indicate either a feeling of helplessness or of unconcern: "Don't ask me, I don't know what to say," or, "I couldn't help it." The shoulder shrug shows that a person feels incapable or uncertain of responding positively to a given situation.

A: Hey, Dave. Why are you shrugging your shoulders at me? All I asked was when Michelle was arriving.

B: Sorry, buddy. I can't say any more. She called a while ago and said she couldn't make it. Something came up at work. She said she'd call back.

A: Okay. Let's run over to the video store and get a good movie for tonight. I'll build a nice fire and we can all relax here at home.

B: You've got it!

37 Winking

Winking is practiced by two people to show a private understanding of a particular situation and to exclude anyone else from the private exchange. In the American cultural arena, winking is also often used to show an appreciation of an attractive person or as an invitation to share the company of the person at whom it is being directed.

A: Sandra, I saw you winking at Jim when you told Tom you'd have dinner with him on the weekend. What's going on?

B: I just wanted Jim to understand that there was nothing serious going on between Tom and me. After all, Jim is my steady beau.

A: Then why did you accept Tom's invitation?

B: He's going off to college, and I wanted to give him a good send-off. You know, we've been friends for many years.

38 Sticking Out Your Tongue

By sticking out their tongues, people react to situations that may be unpleasant for them. Such displays indicate mockery or rejection. For example, children often stick out their tongues to tease each other. Or, they may also stick out their tongues in reaction to activities requiring close concentration; hence, the tongue-showing of children focused on their homework.

A: Does Mark usually concentrate that hard on his homework for school?

B: What made you ask?

A: He really seems intent on solving that math problem. Look how he's sticking out his tongue.

B: True enough. If you think that's something, you should see how he's chewed off the ends of his pencils!

39 Hand over the Mouth When Yawning

Covering the mouth when yawning is considered good manners and stems from two beliefs: first, that covering the mouth safeguarded against the soul's premature departure; second, that an open mouth was an invitation for lurking evil spirits and demons to enter. Now, people still feel strongly about covering the mouth when yawning, possibly for covering up bad breath or even because yawning is contagious.

Jan had been up all night studying for her English finals, and when she came to class she couldn't keep from yawning. It wasn't long before her classmates were all doing the same—much to the consternation of the professor, who was also following their examples.

40 Saying "Bless You" When Sneezing

It was thought in ancient times that when people sneezed they momentarily gave up the Holy Ghost. Thus, during the reign of Pope Gregory the Great, when the population of Rome was overcome by a plague believed to have been caused by contamination of the air, the pope introduced the saying: "God bless you!" to anyone who sneezed. Today, even though a sneeze is considered a symptom of the common cold, and certainly nothing to fear, the expression nevertheless persists.

A: Ah choo!

B: God bless you!

A: Thanks for wishing me well, but unfortunately, I don't think your good wishes are going to help me get rid of this awful cold.

B: I didn't think they would. I'm sure a doctor would be in a better position to help you.

41 The Man Walks on the Outside

When a man and a woman walk together, convention dictates that the man walk on the curb side of the street. The practice probably originated because the man needed to protect his female companion from runaway horses and street brawlers, and from other hazards of the street, such as the garbage being hurled onto the street from upper-story windows.

A: Careful, Kathy. Keep away from the curb or you'll get splashed.

B: I'm sure I'll be well protected from all the elements with you walking next to me. After all, you have always been the perfect gentleman.

A: Thanks for the compliment. I'm glad to see that you appreciate a good man when you see one.

B: Okay, Boris. Don't get carried away.

Part 4
Enjoy!

42 Giving Thanks Before a Meal

The custom of saying prayers before a meal is a result of the belief that God has given us the "grace" to be grateful. Thanking God for the meal we are about to receive is the gratitude we show God for the grace given to us. A prayer of thanks before a meal is a widespread ritual that is an integral part of the many religions practiced in America.

A: What a wonderful dinner you've prepared for the holiday!

B: Thank you. Let's hope it tastes as good as it looks! Now, if you'll all sit down, Dad will say grace before we eat.

A: And let's add a prayer for those less fortunate than we.

43 Keeping Elbows off the Table

Table manners have their origins in the pragmatism of the Middle Ages. The basic idea of keeping elbows off the table is to eat and to let others eat in peace and without friction. People keep their elbows off the table to avoid any close encounters with other elbows or a neighbor's ribs. Just as good fences made good neighbors, arms close to the body make for good table manners.

A: Ouch! Rickie jabbed me with his elbow!

B: Rickie, how many times have I told you to keep your elbows off the table when we're eating?

C: Mom, you just said that it wasn't polite to eat with your elbows on the table. You didn't say anything about paying Tommy back for the poke he gave me before we sat down!

44 Cornflakes for Breakfast

The person responsible for the great American custom of
having cornflakes for breakfast was the vegetarian
health faddist John Harvey Kellogg. Kellogg created the
best-seller of cereals to compete against the evils of
alcohol, tobacco, and malnutrition. Cornflakes, like Coca-
Cola and french fries, became not only one of the salient
characteristics of American culture, but also an eating
habit that invaded the rest of the world.

A: Lucie, don't rush out to school without having your breakfast!
B: But Mom, I feel like having pancakes this morning, but you won't
have time to make them before I go.
A: Well, have your cornflakes for now. They're delicious and
nutritious, and they'll keep you going until lunch. Hotcakes
tomorrow—I promise.

45 Bacon and Eggs

Bacon and eggs (or sometimes sausage or ham) is the traditional American breakfast. It is a throwback to the colonial days when pigs were easy to keep because they could forage for themselves. Eggs for breakfast were ideal because they were at their freshest when gathered from the previous night's roosting. In colonial times pigs and chickens were the easiest animals to transport. Although the opening of the west made beef king, the colonial mania for bacon and eggs persists even after the settling of the west and the end of the frontier.

For years Chris had always eaten a hearty breakfast of bacon and eggs; however, when the doctor told him that he would have to change his diet for health reasons, he didn't take too kindly to having oatmeal instead. After all, he felt that a grown man needed "fitting nourishment" to keep up his strength.

46 Having Salad Before the Entrée

Until about the middle of the nineteenth century, Americans didn't eat salads at all; however, the introduction of the European Waldorf salad shifted the American public's taste toward eating greens. Europeans have their salad after the main course as a way of getting ready to have their cheese. It has been suggested that the American custom of having salad first may be related to the slimming craze of filling up on salad in order to eat less of the main course. Also, restaurants might naturally encourage this practice, since a free salad bar draws the customer's attention away from the meagerness of a meal.

A: Anyone else for more salad?

B: Thanks. Don't mind if I do.

A: My goodness, Mark. Save some room for the entrée. I've prepared a nice pot roast with potatoes for dinner.

B: Don't worry! It'll take much more than salad to make a dent in my appetite. Bring on the roast and let me know what's for dessert.

47 TV Dinners

Along with the advent of television came TV dinners. Because the family no longer seemed to have time for the binding ritual of sitting down together at the dinner table, Swanson and other companies made it possible for the family members to simultaneously watch and eat in front of the TV set. By 1980 the typical TV dinner was twenty minutes long, since the meals were designed to be eaten between the opening and closing of a half-hour program.

A: What's for dinner, Mom?

B: Actually, Dad offered to get dinner tonight. I'm off to my club meeting.

A: Come on. You know that the only thing Dad knows how to prepare is TV dinners. Can't we go out, instead?

B: That's an idea. Since I can't cook, have Dad take you out after your favorite TV show and bring something back for me while you're at it.

48 Ketchup, the American Flavor Marker

It has been suggested that the sauce makes the dish. In 1876 the pickle king, Henry J. Heinz, introduced the blend that today Americans know as ketchup. Heinz produced a sauce derived from a Chinese recipe called *ke tsiap*, which became "ketch op." With the introduction of the tomato and a bit of the culinary innovation, sugar, Heinz capitalized on the public's taste for sweets and made a fortune.

A: And how do you like your burger?
B: Well-done, lettuce, tomato, and no onions.
A: Do you take ketchup or mustard?
B: Ketchup, of course! A burger's not a burger without it. Throw that in for the french fries, too.

49 The Backyard Barbecue

In the 1950s a major incentive for the popularity of the backyard barbecue was probably mom's desire to get out of the kitchen. Nowadays, the barbecue, a mainstream of the suburban lifestyle, is a widespread American custom. It has become not only a culinary event, but a social event as well, where people get together to celebrate national holidays, birthdays, and other special occasions.

A: What's the plan? Are you guys coming over on Sunday to watch the football game?
B: You bet, especially since you're barbecuing. You heat up the coals, and we'll bring the hot dogs and steaks.
A: OK! You're on!

50 Potluck Dinners

On many occasions, when groups of friends or colleagues at work get together for dinner or for a social evening, all the guests offer to contribute something to eat or drink. These dinners are called potluck dinners. They usually consist of a salad or vegetable and several more substantial dishes such as chicken, meatballs, lasagna, or special ethnic delicacies.

Susan was simply overwhelmed with the amount of food that her guests brought to her potluck dinner party. The chicken and lasagna were delightful, but nothing could top the Greek beef *kapama* that Mrs. Eliopoulous contributed. It was the hit of the evening!

51 Eating Fish on Friday

Eating fish on Friday is a survival of a religious custom that goes back to the beginning of Christianity. Jesus and his apostles recommended fasting to accompany prayer as a means of intensifying spiritual insight. The foods prohibited by the custom of abstinence generally were animal flesh and dairy products. Fish, however, was exempted from this structure. In commemoration of the Friday Crucifixion, Friday was designated as the day of denial. Now, although the Vatican has de-emphasized this kind of fasting, people still continue to eat fish on Friday.

A: Hey, Bob. How about coming over for dinner this evening?

B: Sounds good. What are we having?

A: Fish, of course. It's Friday.

B: Great! I'll take you up on that, provided that a salad and a couple of buns go along with the main entrée.

52 Drive-Thru Fast Food

The United States can lay claim to the origination of the fast-food craze. The first fast-food establishments served hamburgers and fried chicken; however, now many other kinds of food are served as well. People may be served inside, where there often is an all-you-can-eat salad bar, or they may order and pick up food without even getting out of the car, at the "drive-thru" section of the restaurant. Fast-food restaurants can now be found worldwide.

A: I feel like getting a burger and fries. There's a fast-food place right around the corner. How about it? You want to drive through or shall we go inside?

B: Let's go in. There's an all-you-can-eat salad bar, and they also serve hot soup.

A: Super! Now that I think of it, I'd like a chocolate shake with my burger. We're in no hurry. We can sit down and relax while we eat.

B: Now you're talkin'. Let's go. It's my treat.

53 Hot Dogs at a Baseball Game

In Germany the hot dog was called the frankfurter. Frankfurters were sold in the United States under the name of "dachshund sausages." These sausages became popular in New York, especially at baseball games. They were sold by men who kept them in hot-water tanks. People ate the dachshund sausages on special breads called buns. One day a cartoonist drew a cartoon of the sausage depicting a dachshund in a roll. Since he didn't know how to spell "dachshund," he wrote "Get Your Hot Dog!" as a caption under the cartoon. Thus, the American hot dog was born.

A: (Voice of a hot-dog vendor at a baseball game) Get your hot dogs! Get your red hots right here!

B: I'll take two—one with relish and mustard and the other one plain.

A: How about a nice cold drink to go with that?

B: OK. A soda would sure hit the spot, and make that a beer for my friend here. That should do it.

Part 5
All in the Family

54 Fall Shopping Sprees

When students return back to school after the summer
vacation, the back-to-school wardrobe is an established
event for starting off the fall semester. Preparations for
returning to school include not only the purchase of fall
fashions at reduced prices, but the stock up on lunch
boxes, book bags, pencils, pens, and notebooks as well.

Rosanne and her sister, Jill, could scarcely restrain their excitement
when their mom informed them she would be taking them shopping
for their fall school wardrobe. They already had combed through the
department stores and knew exactly what they wanted and where to
get it. The only drawback had been the money. Now, thanks to their
generous mom, that little problem would be taken care of.

55 Kiss It and Make It Better

When a child suffers a wound or a scratch, it is common practice to say: "Let Mommie kiss it and make it better." Of course, the parental benefit of kissing a child's injury to "make it go away" has no medical benefit. It is purely a loving gesture to soothe and comfort, to make both parent and child feel better.

A: Ouch!

B: What happened?

A: I accidentally pricked my finger with the needle while I was sewing on this button.

B: Here, let Mom kiss it and make it better.

A: Gee, Mom. It's OK. Save the kiss for something more serious. This is only a scratch.

56 Regular Toothbrushing

In a society where cleanliness and personal hygiene are stressed from early childhood, the practice of brushing three times a day is a standard American ritual. This repetitive behavior is designed to ensure the continuing health of the teeth and gums. The traditional character of this rite is evident in the patient's yearly visit to the dentist to maintain the optimum condition of the mouth.

A: Back from the dentist so soon?
B: Yup. I had a great checkup! No cavities and hardly any plaque.
A: I'm proud of you. I guess that daily brushing really paid off.
B: In more ways than one. No toothaches and a small dental bill!

57 The Tooth Fairy

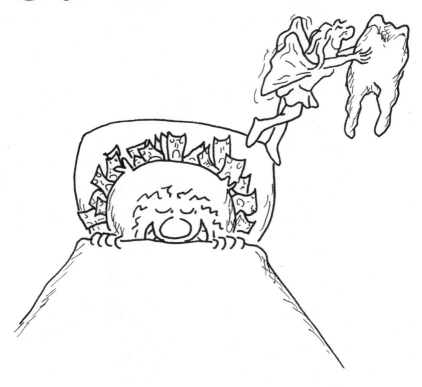

The American children's ritual of hiding a lost tooth under a pillow stems from an old German tradition of placing a lost tooth in a mouse or rat hole so that when a new tooth grew in, it would possess the strong dental qualities of a rodent's tooth. In America the "tooth rat" was replaced by the "tooth fairy," who would compensate the child with money for surrendering a tooth to her.

A: Hey, Mom! Look! My tooth came out!
B: Don't worry, you're fine. We'll put it under your pillow so the tooth fairy can find it. You'll sure be happy in the morning when you find all the money she leaves for you.
A: Hurray! Then we can go to the store and buy something really nice.

58 Sibling Rivalry

Sibling rivalry, arising from competition for parental love and from a natural resentment toward one's rival, is common in American culture. It is an expected rivalry, especially in small families. Parental efforts to stress the importance of sharing one's toys with a brother or sister often fall on deaf ears and cannot overcome a child's innate desire to hold on to what is "his" or "hers" and resentment of any intrusion on his or her property.

Mrs. Jones sure has had her hands full! Between keeping up with the housework and settling arguments between the kids, she was fast coming to the end of her rope. When Mr. Jones offered to get a baby-sitter and take her on an extended weekend getaway, she could scarcely contain her joy.

59 The Weekly Allowance

The modern weekly allowance or "pin money" is a set sum of money that parents give to their children either for entertainment expenses (movies, etc.) or in return for the completion of domestic chores (sweeping, cutting the lawn, taking out the garbage, etc.). This allowance often serves as an early model of money management.

A: I've finally saved enough to get that video game I wanted so badly.
B: Super! I know it costs a small fortune. How did you manage to get your hands on the money?
A: Well, for one thing, I offered to do more work around the house, so my folks upped my weekly allowance. I added to that by doing some yard work for the neighbors. All in all, it was a lot of work, but boy, was it ever worth it!

60 Bedtime Stories

It is a widespread practice for parents to read heavily illustrated stories to their children at bedtime. In doing so, not only do they maintain a practice that was a family tradition before the advent of TV and radio, but they also provide the stimulation so necessary for children's intellectual growth. The practice of one-on-one reading is now more prevalent than ever in America and is strongly endorsed by early childhood educators.

A: Once upon a time there was a beautiful princess who lived in a far-off land.

B: Wait, Mom. Isn't that the story you were reading to me last night?

A: Yes, but you had fallen asleep before I got to the end. Don't you want to know what happened to the princess?

A: Yes, I do, but maybe you could skip the middle part and jump to the end of the story so I'll find out how the story ends before I fall asleep again.

61 An Apple for the Teacher

In the early days of public education, schoolteachers were not salaried and would often be paid in goods and services. Nowadays, presenting an apple to the teacher is interpreted as a gesture of goodwill or as an element of bribery. The practice probably arose from the student's desire to soften the teacher's disposition, thus increasing the student's chances for a more favorable grade. This custom has now given way to parental contributions of money, food, or candy for the enhancement and enrichment of the basic classroom program.

A: Ryan, why are you putting that extra apple in your lunch bag?

B: One is for me and the other is for my math teacher. She really likes apples.

A: Do you suppose that apple might help her see what a brilliant student you are in math?

B: To tell the truth, it couldn't hurt. After all, she might need a little prompting to see the light.

62 Separate Phone Lines for Teens

The teenager's desire for having his or her own phone line apart from the family phone arose from a desire to circumvent other family phone calls and to be able to have private contact with friends for lengthy periods. Now, with the advent of the cellular phone, a private line is readily accessible to anyone who wishes to maintain personal contact with close friends and family alike.

A: Come on, Judy. Hang up. You've been on for over an hour. I'm expecting an important business call.
B: Okay, I'll get off, but I still haven't gotten my own line—like you promised.
A: Look. I'll make a deal with you. I'll get you your own cellular phone and I'll pay the basic monthly cost for the minimum service. Anything over that comes out of your pocket. Agreed?
B: It's a deal!

63 Coupon Clipping

A manufacturer's money-off or reduction coupons appear in all American newspapers and magazines. By purchasing the items that are offered on the reduction coupon, a buyer can have his grocery bill reduced by a substantial amount at the supermarket checkout. Many people plan their grocery shopping in advance to take advantage of the discounts offered by coupons that they collect.

A: My goodness, Ellen! You've got enough groceries there to feed an army!

B: Actually, you wouldn't believe how much we saved by using all those coupons I collected from the Sunday paper and magazines.

A: I must admit you've made a believer out of me. I sincerely apologize for having asked you to stop collecting what I thought was a bunch of junk mail.

B: Now that you've seen the light, you can take me out to dinner with the money that I didn't spend.

64 Garage Sales

Garage sales, or lawn or yard sales, are as big a part of
American culture as apple pie and popcorn. Periodically,
people clean out excess clothing, furniture, appliances,
etc. from their homes and display the goods for sale to
passersby, either on their front lawns or in their garages.
The goods are always sold at greatly reduced prices,
since getting rid of unwanted goods is more important
than realizing even a modest profit from the sales.

A: Louise, what are you planning to do with that old lamp and coffee
table?
B: I hope that I can get a little something for them at the garage sale
I'm planning for this Saturday.
A: Hey, I've got some things I'd like to get rid of, too. How about we do
it together at my place since my garage is bigger?
B: No problem. I'll have my husband clear out the rest of the stuff
from the attic while we're at it.

65 Tupperware Parties

Tupperware parties are gatherings where people display and sell of versatile plastic products to their friends. The products, invented by Earl S. Tupper, were designed to provide people with the necessary conveniences to have the most modern, up-to-date kitchen. Advertising for the products is done by word of mouth. Unlike a store setting, the Tupperware party is personal and lots of fun.

A: Hi, Susan, haven't seen you for a while. What have you been up to?

B: Oh hi, Lisa. Glad I ran into you. I was about to call you and invite you to my Tupperware party on Saturday night.

A: Gee, I'd love to come, but I'll be tied up. Any chance I can get a sneak preview before then?

B: No problem. Come on over this afternoon. I've got all the latest plastic goods on hand and I'd be happy to take your order.

66 Spring Cleaning

Spring cleaning is a major housecleaning project that takes place around March 21, the date of the vernal equinox. After the frost, snow, and debris of the winter months, the advent of warmer weather provides an occasion to clean out the accumulation of the gathered dirt and grit from the past three months. Spring cleaning is a sort of renewal that welcomes in the new season.

Little did Mr. Kowalski imagine how much he let himself in for when he offered to help his wife with spring cleaning. By the time they cleaned the house and emptied out the garage and basement, he felt he deserved a week's vacation; however, in view of the circumstances, a nice evening out would do just fine.

67 Church Collections

The traditional collection of money for the church is an outgrowth of the older custom of presenting gifts to a religious leader in addition to, or in place of, a salary. As the frontier church spread, the preacher passed his hat for money, rather than accept excess grain or other tithes for his services. In time the hat gave way to the modern collection basket or tray lined with velvet or felt to muffle the clink of dropped coins or paper money.

Thanks to the financial support of the parishioners, the new youth center was well on its way to completion. The overwhelming response to the request for contributions for the center, in addition to the generous Sunday offerings placed in the collection tray, made possible the realization of this dream.

Part 6
Let's Have Fun!

68 A Game of Bingo

The game of bingo is an ongoing American custom that is encouraged by civic groups, and is condoned by the church as well, in exchange for the needed income the game provides. It is customary for players to get together in an atmosphere free from the chaos of modern society and where they can interact on a social, congenial basis. Since the stakes are usually a dollar a card, bingo is considered a low-risk game and thus poses no threat of economic difficulties for the players.

For a couple of years now, ever since he retired, Jack and his wife have been regular players at the Saturday night bingo games held in their church hall. Although they don't win very often, they nevertheless enjoy getting together with their friends to catch up on the weekly gossip and to go out afterward for coffee and pie.

69 Square Dancing

Although the square dance is mainly associated with the American cowboy, it is a traditional dance enjoyed by many people throughout the United States. It is customary for the men to dress in a traditional cowboy outfit and for the women to wear lace blouses and full skirts. Four couples form a square and a caller shouts out what movements they need to make.

A: I haven't had so much fun in a long time. I danced until I was ready to drop!

B: Did you go dancing at that new ballroom auditorium downtown?

A: No. We went to a square dance on a ranch right outside of town. You should have seen Bill in his cowboy outfit and me in my skirt and blouse. We danced up a real storm!

B: Sounds like you had a great time. Let me know the next time you go. I could use the exercise.

70 Going to a Rodeo

In the nineteenth century, the cowboys who worked on big ranches in the West spent weeks rounding up cattle and taking them to the markets or the railway yards. At the end of a roundup, they held competitions called rodeos to see who was best at roping a cow, riding a wild horse, or shooting. Rodeos are big affairs with bands, singing cowboys, and clowns providing entertainment. They are still popular today, with around 500 taking place in the United States each year.

A: Boy, you have to roll with the blows to be able to stay on a horse when it's bucking so hard.

B: How about the guys who get dragged all over the place trying to rope those steers? Now, that's something to see!

A: And don't forget the clowns and the lively band music.

B: Isn't that what a rodeo is all about? Fun and entertainment for all!

71 Demolition Derbies

Demolition derbies are large-scale automobile rodeos that take place in large arenas. The entrants pay a fee to drive their dilapidated autos into each other, and the last car moving is declared the winner. Demolition derbies reflect the Americans' fascination with cars and provide a form of entertainment whose main appeal is that of wanton destruction.

A: I'm off to the central arena for the demolition derby. Want to come along?

B: No, thanks. As it is, I get upset thinking about all the car wrecks that take place on the highways. I'm in no mood for witnessing more.

A: Don't be such a wet blanket. No one gets hurt—it's all in fun.

B: Not so for the guy whose car gets hammered.

72 A Visit to the Amusement Park or Theme Park

Americans love amusement parks. From the Ferris wheels, pie-eating contests, and livestock exhibits of county and state fairs, to the gigantic roller coasters and water slides of regional theme parks, to the world-famous Disney World and Disneyland, many American families visit amusement parks for a summer vacation treat.

A: Hi, Jimmy. Back so soon from Disneyland?

B: Yup. We had a great time! Especially my dad—he was like a little kid going on the Matterhorn and on all those other rides.

A: That's great to hear. Our family's planning to go there next week, but we can only stay for two days.

B: That's OK. You'll still have a ball!

73 Eating Contests

The eating contest is a tried-and-true American custom practiced at state fairs and ethnic festivals around the country. It is a kind of eat-until-you-bust affair at which the contestants gorge themselves on regional delicacies (often kielbasa or pie) to compete for prizes. The contests are popular affairs where the axiom "more is better" seems to be the order of the day.

A: Unbelievable! He's already on his third pie, and still going strong.
B: If you think that's something, the guy next to him is already working on his fourth and with a whipped-cream topping to boot.
A: I'm betting the first guy'll win. That second guy already looks under the weather. I don't see how he can last.
B: It looks like you're right. Look! Now he's turning green!

74 TGIF (Thank Goodness It's Friday)

This day finds people from all walks of life frequenting restaurants, bars, and taverns for drink and nourishment to release the tension of the five-day workweek and perhaps to replenish their energies for the coming week. An adjunct to TGIF is the happy hour, when drinks and appetizers in cocktail lounges and bars are served at reduced prices.

A: After such a stressful week I'm really looking forward to our Friday outing.

B: Are we still going to the same place on Market Street?

A: Sure, why not? It's a great place to relax. Inexpensive drinks, appetizers of all kinds, and congenial friends. What more could you want to recharge your battery?

B: How about winning the lottery?

75 Tailgate Parties

Tailgate parties are now an established American custom that take place before a sports event, such as a football or basketball game. The fans congregate around the tailgate of a truck or the back end of a sedan or sports utility vehicle and celebrate the upcoming game with food, drink, and animated conversations in support of their favorite team. The parties are boisterous events that promote conviviality among the participants and elevate the spirits of the fans before the game.

A: Mary, is all the food ready to go?

B: Yeah, it's all set. Just get it in the van, and I'll bring the drinks.

A: We'd better get going. We're supposed to meet the Smiths for tailgating in the main parking lot of the stadium at 11 o'clock.

B: Fine. But what's your hurry? The game doesn't start until two.

A: Come on, Mary. Where's your spirit? We've got to cheer on our team, and we sure can't do it on empty stomachs.

76 Baseball— America's Game

One of the most distinctly American institutions is the game of baseball. The game is avidly followed by a great number of fans, either attending in person or watching on TV. Most of the time, the spectator's attention is focused on the batter and the pitcher. The game is not only practiced on a professional level, but on a local, suburban level as well.

The baseball stadium was packed with the fans rooting for their team at the championship game. In the bottom of the ninth inning with the score tied, a member of the home team hit the ball clear out of the stadium. Pandemonium broke loose as the fans roared their approval. But the best part was yet to come. Because of their victory, the members of the team not only received the accolades of the mayor and jubilant fans in a ticker tape parade, but healthy bonuses as well.

77 Playing on Little League Teams

Little League teams are baseball and softball teams for boys and girls from ages 8 to 12. Thousands belong to these teams. Many families and groups of friends get together on weekends and on holidays and play baseball or softball in parks and in spacious lots. After the game there is often a picnic or a barbecue.

A: Come one, Dad, let's get going. I've got to warm up my pitching arm before we start playing.

B: OK, Jimmy, I'm on my way. I'm just getting the treats ready for all you Little Leaguers for after the game.

A: Be sure you bring enough. You know how hungry the guys get after playing so hard.

B: No problem. Win or lose, we're all going out for pizza right after the game. You can eat to your hearts' content.

78 Listening to One's Favorite Music

In addition to rock and standard pop music, throughout the United States people can hear many forms of music that the Americans have given to the world. Jazz, blues, soul, and rap have all originated from African-American culture. Also, enjoying great popularity is country and western music, coming from traditional folk music. The Grand Old Opry in Nashville, Tennessee, is the center for this music.

A: Say, Matt. Look here in the paper. The Metallic Munchers rock group is going to be in town for a concert on the weekend. Want to go?

B: To tell you the truth, the Metallic Munchers aren't exactly my cup of tea. I'm more into jazz and blues. Why not ask Diane to go? That's right up her alley.

A: I think I'll take you up on that.

B: You won't be sorry. She's really into that kind of music. You'll be better off with her than you'd ever be with me!

79 Lighting Matches at a Rock Concert

The custom of the audience lighting matches at a well-received rock concert was invented by appreciative fans of the 1960s rock stars. The ritual was initiated by a grateful audience as a method of paying tribute to the musicians. It is thought that perhaps the light of the match or lighter is appropriate to the rock medium since to many people rock performers have become like high priests of this musical idiom.

A: That was some concert! But tell me, why is everybody lighting matches?

B: Well, it's a kind of tribute to the musicians. The group has been performing for a number of years, and it's still going strong. For their fans, they're practically like earthly gods.

A: Gee! I wonder what Beethoven would have thought of all this?

Part 7
Red Letter Days

80 Honoring Martin Luther King's Birthday

On January 15 the people of the United States celebrate the birthday of Martin Luther King Jr., a civil rights leader who fought against racial discrimination in the 1960s. He said that people should be judged by their character and not by the color of their skin. On this day people listen to his speeches, watch TV documentaries, and sing the civil rights anthem "We Shall Overcome."

A: Hi, Eric. You know, today's the fifteenth of the month. How about coming over with Loretta to honor King's birthday? I have some videos of the speeches he gave during those years of turmoil.

B: That would work out well for us since we have no other definite plans. By the way, there's also a documentary on TV tracing the beginnings of the civil rights movement.

A: Wonderful. Let's make an evening out of it. We'll be expecting you as soon as you can get here. Dinner's on us.

81 Celebrating Mardi Gras

Mardi Gras, which is French for "Fat Tuesday" (the Tuesday before Lent), is a gala festival that takes place early in the year in New Orleans, Louisiana. The festival, or Carnival, closely resembles the wildness of New Year's Eve celebrations. The terms *Mardi Gras* and *Carnival* refer to the period of festivity that preceded Lent in the medieval church calendar. The carnival season is usually about ten days long with big parades, parties, and dances. When the parades pass by, people holler to the paraders to throw them something. Then everyone fights to catch the small presents thrown to them.

A: Don, what a pleasant surprise! What brings you to New Orleans this time of year?

B: Actually, I came on business, but I'm going to be staying on for Mardi Gras.

A: Good. We can watch the parade together, and we can go to my place after for drinks and something to eat.

B: Sounds great! Now I know what people mean when they talk about that famous Southern hospitality.

82 Presidents' Day Sales

On the third Monday in February, the people of the United States honor two great presidents, George Washington and Abraham Lincoln. George Washington, "Father of His Country," was the commander in chief of the Continental Army that won the thirteen original colonies' independence from Great Britain in the Revolutionary War. Abraham Lincoln was able to unite the country during the period of American history when seven Southern states tried to break away from the Union and start their own country. He is also praised for the proclamation that ended slavery in all parts of the United States. As with other legal holidays, it is customary for retail stores to have sales on Presidents' Day.

A: Do you have Presidents' Day off on Monday?

B: Sure do, and I need the break!

A: Doing anything special?

B: I plan to go car shopping. This is the perfect time to do it. All of the car dealers are having fabulous sales on leasing and on buying.

A: You can't go wrong on a day like that. Why don't you drive by after you've gotten "the deal of deals" and let me see what you've picked up?

83 Wearing Green on Saint Patrick's Day

Saint Patrick is the patron saint of Ireland, and many people in the United States commemorate this day (March 17) by wearing something green, the color that is traditionally associated with Ireland. There is a big gala parade in New York City, and millions of real shamrocks flown in from Ireland are used for decorations. Green balloons and green and gold peanuts are sold by the hundreds. Shops prepare green pasta, green ice cream, and green bread, and people drink Irish coffee and sing Irish songs throughout the day.

A: How do you like my new sweater?

B: Very becoming. I especially like that shade of green. What's the occasion?

A: I thought I'd kill two birds with one stone. First of all, I needed a new sweater and, of course, since Saint Patrick's Day is coming up, I thought I'd get it in green.

B: Good thinking. Now all you need are the shoes and skirt to go with it. Green, of course?

A: Of course.

84 Sending Flowers on Mother's Day

Mother's Day is celebrated on the second Sunday in May. It was the idea of a West Virginia schoolteacher. Upon observing the ill treatment of many elders by their children, she undertook a writing campaign, petitioning businessmen and congressmen to set aside a day in the year to honor mothers. It is now the custom for children to give their mothers cards, flowers, or presents on this day. Mother's Day is also a day when many people attend religious services to honor parents who have passed away.

Although the children were all grown up and living away from home, they never failed to send flowers and get together to take Mom out for dinner on Mother's Day. For Mom, however, the meal was a bonus. The main course was the love and devotion her children showed her year after year on this special day.

85 Wearing a Poppy for Memorial Day

Memorial Day, also called Decoration Day, is a patriotic holiday to honor the dead of all wars, officially celebrated on the last Monday in May. It is a national celebration, a day of parades, oratorical elegies, and wreath laying. People place flowers, flags, and artificial poppies on the graves of servicemen and servicewomen. The artificial poppy has become the symbol of the tragedy of World War I, since many of the battlefields of France bloomed with poppies.

A: Come on, Grandpa! It's almost time for the parade.

B: I'm almost ready. I just have to pin on my red poppy and I'll be set to go.

A: But why are you wearing a poppy?

B: It's in memory of all those who served our country and who, unfortunately, never returned. To honor our brave soldiers is one of the reasons for today's Memorial Day parade.

A: Gee, Grandpa. I'm sure glad that you came back from the wars. I guess that means I won't ever have to wear a red poppy. Right?

86 Independence Day Parade

On July 4, 1776, the United States declared its independence from England. In honor of this great day in history, Americans celebrate Independence Day, commonly called the Fourth of July, every year on that day. Families and friends get together on the day for parades, picnics, barbecues, and fireworks extravaganzas.

A: Will you be going to see the fireworks tonight?

B: Wouldn't miss it! Jan and I will be spending the day at the picnic grounds with some relatives and we'll watch the fireworks from there.

A: Listen, after the picnic, why don't you come over to our place? We will have a great view of the fireworks from our balcony and we can keep on enjoying the day with some snacks and a couple of drinks.

B: Okay. If it's no bother, I've got to admit, it'll be great spending the day with friends.

87 "Trick or Treat" on Halloween

Halloween, also referred to as All Hallow's Eve, falls on October 31. It is believed that on this day, ghosts, spirits, and witches come out to harm people. In order to scare the evil spirits away, people place scary decorations such as black cats, skeletons, and ghosts in front of their homes. Children dressed in masks and colorful costumes go from door to door saying "trick or treat," and people give them candy, cookies, fruit, or money.

A: Let's get going, Judy. It's already getting dark. Sue is expecting us for trick or treating tonight.

B: I'll be right there. By the way, are you still going dressed as a wicked witch?

A: Absolutely. And how about you?

B: Probably just as myself. I don't have a costume.

A: That should frighten a lot of people and get you a lot of treats. Mind sharing them with me?

88 Voting on Election Day

Election Day, a legal holiday, is held on the Tuesday after the first Monday in November. On this day American citizens elect their public officials, president, congressional representatives, governors, mayors, and judges, and vote on issues of public interest. On the night of the election, people watch the election results on TV and listen to the speeches made by the winning candidates. As on other legal holidays, Election Day sales in stores are very popular.

A: Al, I might be coming in late for work tomorrow. I'm stopping by my polling place to vote.

B: Oh yeah, tomorrow's Election Day. The date slipped my mind.

A: How could you forget? All the TV commercials have been about the candidates. Their posters are plastered on everyone's lawn.

B: I was kidding when I said the date slipped my mind. I'm just upset with the candidates' debates preempting my favorite TV programs. To tell you the truth, I'll be glad when this whole thing is over.

89 Gathering for Thanksgiving Dinner

Thanksgiving is celebrated throughout the United States on the fourth Thursday in November with a large feast of turkey with stuffing, sweet potatoes, cranberry sauce, and pumpkin pie for dessert. When the Pilgrims, seeking religious freedom, first came to American shores from England, they endured many hardships. Native Americans taught them how to survive. As a token of gratitude, the Pilgrims invited their Native American friends to share a feast with them. This was the first Thanksgiving and was celebrated in 1621, a year after the arrival of the Pilgrims to Plymouth Rock, in Massachusetts.

A: That turkey sure smells good! When's dinner?

B: Be patient. Aunt Sally is due to arrive any minute with the salad and pumpkin pies, and Uncle Ned'll be here real soon with the refreshments.

A: I can hardly wait!

B: Just take it easy and remember don't let your eyes be bigger than your stomach. Remember how you felt last year when you overate?

A: No problem. This year I have a bigger stomach.

90 Celebrating Kwanza

Kwanza, a Swahili word for "the first fruits of the harvest," is a celebration of African-American culture inspired by African harvest festivals. The celebration originated in America and begins on December 26. It lasts for seven days and centers on seven African practices encompassing, among others, ideals of unity, self-determination, and faith. Each evening the family lights one of seven candles, exchanges gifts, and discusses the principle for the day. Near the end of the holiday the community gathers for a feast and enjoys many original culinary dishes.

A: What are you all doing after your Kwanza ceremony tonight?

B: After we light the last candle and exchange gifts, we're heading over to Antonetta's house for a potluck feast. Want to come along?

A: I'd be happy to. Just wait till you taste my Creole bread pudding! It's out of this world!

Part 8
The Icons of America

91 Visiting the Statue of Liberty

A visit to the Statue of Liberty is an inspiring experience for both Americans and immigrants. It was a gift from the French people to commemorate the hundredth birthday of the United States, since France had helped the American colonies gain their independence from England during the Revolutionary War. For the many immigrants who come to the United States through New York, the Statue of Liberty, holding up her torch, symbolizes a welcome to a land of freedom and possibilities for a better life.

A: We're finally in New York. What's the first thing on the agenda for today?

B: I'd like to take in the view of the city from the Empire State Building.

A: Before we do that, I think a visit to the Statue of Liberty should take first priority. After all, it represents what America is all about.

B: I'll go for that, but I'd still like to check out downtown Manhattan and visit some of those fancy stores along 5th Avenue.

92 Taking in a Broadway Show

When in New York City, it is customary for the visitor to take in a Broadway show. Broadway is a main thoroughfare in Manhattan. It is here and on neighboring streets that the newest plays and the biggest and brightest musicals are presented. These are some of the best shows in the world, and invariably go on tour to theaters across the country and abroad.

A: I'm so excited! I was able to get tickets for the latest Broadway musical!

B: That'll be the high point of our visit to New York. But tell me, were they expensive?

A: They cost an arm and a leg, but it'll be worth it. After all, "man does not live by bread alone."

93 Stargazing in Hollywood

Hollywood, an area in the city of Los Angeles, is the mainstay of the American movie industry. Nearly all important American movie studios are located in Hollywood, where many famous and glamorous movie stars reside. Today, many movies are made outside of Hollywood, but visitors to Hollywood can go to the famous Chinese Theatre and see the footprints and autographs of many favorite movie stars.

A: Hi, Silvia. How was your trip to Hollywood?

B: It was very exciting, especially the tour we took to the houses of the movie stars. What mansions!

A: And did you see any real, live movie stars?

B: The closest we came was the footprints and autographs at Mann's Chinese Theatre. But maybe next time. Where there's life, there's hope.

94 Enjoying Popcorn at the Movies

Native Americans ate popcorn as food and were the first to try it popped. It was not until 1914 that a farm boy from Iowa formed the American Pop Corn Company and began to sell popcorn. Gradually, it became a national fad. In the 1920s it was introduced into the movie theaters. People wanted to eat it during the movie, but the theater managers discouraged the practice since the crunching distracted the other patrons. With the introduction of background music and sound for the movies, which drowned out the crunching, coupled with the need for cash during the Depression, the theater managers had a change of heart and permitted the establishment of lobby concessions. Popcorn is now an established "must" for all theatergoers.

A: Hold on a second. I want to get my bag of popcorn.
B: But look at the big line at the concession stand. You're liable to miss the beginning of the movie.
A: It doesn't matter. I can't watch the movie without my popcorn.
B: OK. I'll go find us a seat. You bring the popcorn. And don't forget a couple of Cokes while you're at it.

95 Ordering an Ice-Cream Cone

The prototype for modern American ice cream was the Roman concoction of cream mixed with berries and alpine snow. The treat made it to America in the 1740s and soon took off rapidly in the colonies. By the nineteenth century America was thoroughly taken in with the treat. It first appeared on a cone when a vendor at the St. Louis World's Fair ran out of the dishes in which he was serving the ice cream and began serving it in cone-shaped waffles, which he obtained from a vendor of *zalabia*, a Persian-style waffle. There is nothing more American than an ice-cream cone, or a hot dog, and a Coke at a sports event or theater.

A: That was a great meal. How about topping it off with an ice-cream cone?

B: Super! Let's go to Dave's Ice Cream Shoppe. He serves a ton of flavors. So, what flavor are you going to have?

A: Probably licorice.

B: Yuck. I'm going to go with vanilla. As a matter of fact, I'll probably have a big scoop in a cup with a little chocolate syrup. Nothing like sticking with the old tried-and-true.

96 Chewing Gum

An American inventor, Thomas Adams, bought some chicle (gum resin) from a Mexican dictator and sold it as gum balls to a candy store in New Jersey. At a time when tobacco chewing was ever popular in America, the gum balls caught on quickly and the chewing gum industry was born. In the 1890s William Wrigley made the gum into flat sticks and added special flavors. Today Wrigley's Spearmint gum and Juicy Fruit gum are among the most popular in America. During the war American soldiers overseas gave the gum to people they met. Thus, gum became as popular all over the world as it was in the United States.

A: Elena, how many times must I tell you not to chew gum in class?

B: I can't help it. I get nervous when I'm taking an exam, and it calms my nerves.

A: It seems to me that if you studied harder you wouldn't get so nervous. Just don't go back to biting your nails, OK?

97 Having a Coke

Coca-Cola is an American classic refreshment. It was originally made from a syrup of coca leaves and cola nuts and sold as a medicine. A pharmacist added soda water to the concoction and made the drink available to the consumer in ready-to-drink bottles and in soda fountains. Eventually, the soda fountain gave way to the modern soda pop machine, which dispenses not only Coke but other popular soft drinks as well.

A: I'm so hot! Let's get a Coke. There's a pop machine right outside that store over there.

B: What would you like?

A: I'll have a Diet Sprite.

B: OK, a nice cold Diet Sprite coming up for you and a regular Pepsi for me. Now all I need is four more quarters and we can be on our way.

98 The Morning Cup of Coffee

Coffee drinking had been going on in the colonies since 1670. During the War of 1812, British tea became unavailable, and it was then that coffee took over. By the 1800s coffee, once the exclusive property of the East, was most successfully produced in Brazil; so Americans didn't have to drink tea, whether brought in by the British or anyone else. Since then, few Americans can start the day without a cup of coffee.

A: Boy, that coffee sure smells good! How about a cup?

B: Help yourself.

A: Thanks. It'll help me start my day. I've got to stay awake and alert for my sales presentation to the board. Aren't you having any?

B: I've already had three cups. If I have any more I won't be able to sleep tonight.

A: Well then, we can go out and paint the town red. What do you say?

99 As American as Apple Pie

The apple pie did not originate in America. English colonists brought a taste for the fruit from the Old World and began planting orchards as early as 1625. Dried, raw, and cooked, the apple found its way into numerous colonial dishes. Apple pie became known as American, not because it was invented in America, but because of the abundance of apples in the orchards of Washington and New York. No other dessert is more identifiable with America than apple pie.

A: What's for desert?

B: Mom baked an apple pie.

A: Yum, my favorite. Are we having it à la mode or with cheddar cheese?

A: You can have yours with ice cream. I'll have mine plain because I'm on a diet, although I wouldn't object to having a nice big piece since it's homemade and fresh.

100 Wearing Blue Jeans

The wearing of blue jeans is now an established American mode of dress for men and women alike. Jeans are considered not just practical, but very fashionable as well. It all began with Levi Strauss, an immigrant from Germany. He arrived in San Francisco in 1850, in the middle of the Gold Rush. He thought the miners could use strong pants, so he took some canvas and made it into jeans. Eventually, he used a softer fabric called denim, which he dyed blue to give the pants a more interesting look. Today the company he started is known around the world.

A: What are you wearing to the art exhibition? I understand it's going to be a rather high-class affair.

B: My blue jeans with a white shirt, tie, and a sport coat.

A: Do you think jeans would be appropriate for the occasion?

B: Sure. Why not? If those designers of men's clothes can wear them at fashion shows and on TV guest appearances, I'm sure I'll fit right in. It's not like I'm going to be best man at somebody's wedding.

101 Reading Personal Advice Columns

Personal advice columns, especially the ones that deal with problems of the heart, enjoy an overwhelming popularity in America. The current strong interest in personal questions represents a break with the tradition of readers being more interested in religion and natural sciences rather than in affairs of the heart. Personal advice columns not only appear in most major newspapers, but can also be heard on many radio stations.

A: Did you read Adele's advice to that young girl who said that she was in love and wanted to marry some guy who had no job?

B: I sure did! She was even willing to abandon her studies for her teaching credential in midstream just to run off with this loser.

A: Adele was right in advising her to get that credential before she even thought about marriage.

B: Absolutely! She would be going out on a limb placing her trust in someone who would hardly be able to support her. How can love thrive without the means to keep it alive?

Index

A

allowance 70
amusement park 85
anniversary gifts 33
apple for the teacher 72
apple pie 117
asking for a woman's hand
  26

B

bachelor party 28
back to school 65
backyard barbecue 58
bacon and eggs 54
baptism 6
bar (bat) mitzvah 11
baseball 89, 90, 62
basketball 88
bedtime stories 71
bingo 81
birthday 7, 8, 9
birthday cake and candles
  9
birthday spankings 8
"bless you" 47
blue is for boys 4
blue jeans 118
boys 4
breakfast 53, 54
bridal shower 27
bride 26, 27, 29, 30
bride's family paying for
  the wedding 29
Broadway show 110

C

caps and gowns 14

card 18
Carnival 96
chewing gum 114
church collections 78
cigars 5
cleaning 77
Coca-Cola, Coke 115
coffee 116
Communion 10
cornflakes 53
country music 91
coupon clipping 74
cowboy 83, 82
crossing fingers 41
crossing heart 42
cutting wedding cake 32

D

dance 16, 25, 82
date 16, 23
Decoration Day 100
demolition derbies 84
dentist 67
Depression 112
diamond 33
dinner 56, 59
Disney World 85
dowry 27, 29
drive-thru fast food 61
Dutch treat 24

E

eating contests 86
eating fish on Friday 60
eggs 54
elbows 52
Election Day 103

entrée 55
equinox 77

F
fall shopping sprees 65
fast food 61
fingers 41
First Communion 10
fish 60
flowers 99
football 88
Fourth of July 101
frankfurter 62
Friday 60, 87

G
garage sales 75
girls 4
giving thanks 51
giving the bride away 26
going Dutch 24
gold 33
gown 14
graduation 14
grace 51
Grand Old Opry 91
green 98
greeting cards 18
gum 114

H
Halloween 102
hamburgers 61
hand in marriage 26
hand over mouth 46
happy hour 87
hazing 13
heart 42
Heinz, Henry J. 57
high five 40

Hollywood 111
homecoming 15
hot dogs 62

I
ice-cream cone 113
Independence Day 101
Irish 98

J
jeans 118
July 4 101

K
ketchup 57
keeping elbows off table 52
Kellogg, John Harvey 53
King, Jr., Martin Luther 95
kiss it and make it better 66
kiss the bride 30
kissing 12, 21, 22, 23, 30, 66
Kwanza 105

L
lawn sales 75
leap year 25
lighting matches 92
Lincoln, Abraham 97
Little League teams 90
Los Angeles 111

M
Manhattan 110
Mardi Gras 96
marking X for kisses 21
Memorial Day 100

Mother's Day 99
movies 112
music 91, 92

N
Nashville 91
Native Americans 104,
    112
New Orleans 96
New York City 98, 109,
    110
newspapers 74

O
OK sign 38

P
parade 15, 101
parking with a date 23
parties 12, 76
passing out cigars 5
personal advice columns
    119
Pilgrims 104
pink is for girls 4
popcorn 112
poppy 100
potluck dinners 59
Presidents' Day 97
prom 16

R
retirement watch 17
rice 31
rock concert 92
rodeo 83

S
Sadie Hawkins dance 25
Saint Patrick's Day 98

salad 55
sale 75, 97
separate phone lines 73
shaking hands 37
shamrock 98
shopping 65
shoulders 43
shower 27
shrugging shoulders 43
sibling rivalry 69
singing Happy Birthday 7
sixteen 12
sneezing 47
softball 90
spanking 8
spin the bottle 22
spring cleaning 77
square dance 82
stag party 28
stargazing in Hollywood
    111
Statue of Liberty 109
sticking out tongue 45
stories 71
stork 3
Strauss, Levi 118
Swanson 56
sweet sixteen 12

T
tailgate parties 88
teacher 72
teens 73
telephone 73
TGIF, Thank Goodness It's
    Friday 87
Thanksgiving 104
theme park 85
thumbs up/down 39
tongue 45

tooth fairy 68
toothbrushing 67
trick or treat 102
Tupper, Earl S. 76
Tupperware parties 76
turnabout dance 25
TV dinner 56

V
Vatican 60
visit from the stork 3
voting 103

W
walking on the outside 48
Washington, George 97

watch 17
wearing blue jeans
   118
wearing green 98
wedding 29, 30, 31
wedding cake 32
weekly allowance 70
winking 44
Wrigley, William 114

X
X for kisses 21

Y
yard sales 75
yawning 46